# VIVID

## POEMS & NOTES ABOUT COLOR

## JULIE PASCHKIS

HENRY HOLT AND COMPANY • NEW YORK

For Stephen Iino

Yellow is often described as the color most visible to humans. Because many birds and insects can see ultraviolet light (such as light from X-rays or the sun), it is likely that birds and insects are especially sensitive to the brightness of yellow light. And the yolk of an egg turns a deeper yellow if a chicken eats more yellow plants. (Cardinals also turn redder if they eat more red foods, including seeds or berries, and flamingos turn pink from eating shrimp.)

# YELLOW

Loudly, rowdy
daffodils yell hello.
Hot yellow.

The color orange is named after the fruit orange. Until the early sixteenth century there was no word for the color orange in English. The Himba tribe of Namibia still has no word for orange.

# ORANGE

Orange you sweet?
Orange you plump and juicy?
Orange you my favorite fruit?
Hey—you're a tangerine!
B-lime-y.

Even though there are many words for colors, there are still more colors than there are words to describe them. You are less likely to see a color if you don't have a name for it.

Since ancient times, red paints have been made from rust and also from cochineal insects—bugs that live on cactus plants.

# RED

Inquired Patrice:

"What color paint would you like tonight?
Crimson, scarlet, or cadmium light?

Magenta, madder, beet, carmine?
Quinacridone rose, alizarin?

There are a zillion!
Even vermilion!"

"Red," said Fred.

Lots of expressions include colors: feeling BLUE, tickled PINK, telling a WHITE lie. Why? Why are you GREEN with envy instead of ORANGE with envy?

# RED TO PINK

Jack, in the red,
sold old brown cow
for three green beans.
Felt blue.
Black magic or green thumb?
Beans grew.
Phew.
Up, up slow.
Fee. Fi. Fo.
Ogre grim.
Fum.
White lie.
Jack didn't die.
Got bold.
Stole gold.
Quick, think!
Down in a wink.
Jack, tickled pink.

The color pink was named after a flower (pinks, also called the dianthus plant or Sweet William). In the 1920s pink was considered a color for boys. Red is a forceful color, and pink suggested masculinity because it is light red. In the 1940s pink switched to being associated with girls. Pink is for everyone now.

# PINK

Tulips press together—
a soft spring kiss.
Pink bliss.

Violet is the color with the shortest wavelength
of visible light. In ancient times Tyrian purple dye
was made of sea snails in Phoenicia, now Lebanon.
It took about 243,000 snails to make one ounce of
dye. The dye sold for three times its weight in gold.
Only kings and queens could afford to wear purple.

# PURPLE

I'm a Lilac Point Siamese
with no fleas.
Watch my tail twitch and flick.
Pounce! My paws are quick.
I lick them languidly.
I'm slow, silken, fluid, fast.
My cool eyes like glass
look past you.
I purr:
I'm not *purr*ple.
I'm a lilac queen,
serene.

Water molecules absorb red, orange, and yellow
light. They reflect most of the blue and green light
that enters them. That is why bodies of water look
blue. Deeper into the water, less light can get through
the molecules. Deep under the sea it is as dark as night.

# INDIGO

Diving
into
Long Lake
headfirst
in I go
plummeting
through
light
blue
deep
down
low
into
indigo.

Even though blue is often associated
with sadness, it is the most popular
color, according to polls taken in
ten countries around the world.

**BLUE**

Oh, what did I do?
Blue-hoo,
Blue-hoo!

The word *green* in English comes
from *grene*—and further back, from
*grōwan*, which is the same origin
as for the words *grass* and *grow*.

# GREEN

Green smell of a summer lawn.
Damp dawn long gone.
Green song of a summer lawn.
In the hot sun I hum along.

There are more green plants than there are plants of any other color. Plants look green because they contain chlorophyll, which absorbs most of the red and blue light and some yellow while reflecting green.

Some animals take on a green color to hide in the green plants—camouflage!

# GREENS

Eat your greens!

The hungry dragon says:
"Mmm—small and scaly.
I'll gobble one daily."

The hungry ogre says:
"Mmm—large and scaly.
I'll start with the tail-y."

Synesthesia is when you experience one sense with a different sense. For example, you might smell a color or see a sound. The artist Georgia O'Keeffe experienced synesthesia and used to hum the colors that she painted.

# BROWN

Lost in the woods.
Brown branches all around,
around.
Brown sounds—
hoot, scurry, crunch,
and creak.
Growls
Owls
O.

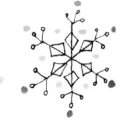

Color comes to your eyes through light waves
of different lengths. Snow looks white because
all the light waves bounce off the ice crystals
in the snow and combine to make white.

Black is the absence of light. Certain animals
that are awake at night don't need to see bright
colors. Some microbats can't see bright colors
at all—but they can clearly distinguish black,
white, and shades of gray.

## WHITE

Black turns into white.
Grandmother's hair.

## BLACK

White turns into black.
Snow melting on
pavement.

Rainbows are made by the reflection and refraction (bending) of light in drops of water.

Rainbows are actually full circles though they look like arcs from the ground.

# RAINBOW

Under the hot honey sun
I ate a rainbow picnic.

Corn and beans.
Collard greens.
Blueberry pie.
Sigh.
Purple plums and huckleberries.
Watermelon, juicy cherries.
Ripe red tomatoes cut thick.
Carrot sticks.
Golden apples, sun dappled.
Tart lemonade—cool sips.
Snowy white ice cream.
Slow licks, drips.

I slurped. I burped.

And now, in the cool gray shade,
a nap
with vivid dreams.

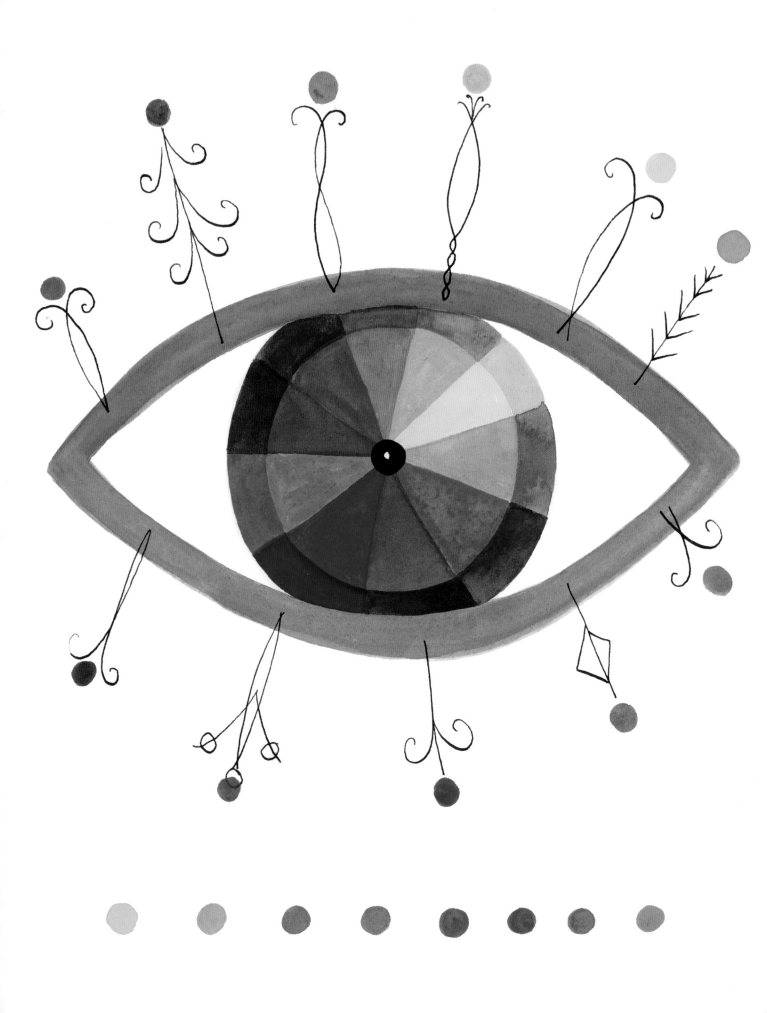

# AUTHOR'S NOTE

The world is full of color. We take in the world through our eyes. Color is woven into language. Colors are connected to our moods.

Colors mean different things in different societies. Colors look different alone than they do next to one another.

But what is color?

The science of color is complicated. There are two different systems of color. We see color as light. All the colors of the rainbow are made of light of different wavelengths and particles that bounce off objects and reflect back into our eyes. If you mix all the colors of light together, you see white.

A different kind of color is used in painting, dyeing, and printing. Those colors are pigments made from various materials such as plants, insects, minerals, and chemical compounds. If you mix all those colors together, you get a dark, muddy mess.

Color depends on perception. Dogs see blue and yellow but not green and red. Many fish can see ultraviolet light. Some people are color blind and can't tell red from green. Other people are especially sensitive to color. Birds, reptiles, and butterflies can see more colors than any person can. Mantis shrimp can detect the most colors. Do you see what someone else sees?

In this book I paint poems of different colors, and I include some colorful facts and questions. I hope it inspires you to explore the art and science of color: to write, read, and draw a blue streak!

Henry Holt and Company, *Publishers since 1866*
Henry Holt® is a registered trademark of Macmillan Publishing Group, LLC
175 Fifth Avenue, New York, NY 10010  •  mackids.com

Library of Congress Control Number: 2017957946
ISBN 978-1-250-12229-2

Our books may be purchased in bulk for promotional,
educational, or business use. Please contact your local
bookseller or the Macmillan Corporate and Premium Sales
Department at (800) 221-7945 ext. 5442 or by e-mail at
MacmillanSpecialMarkets@macmillan.com.

First edition, 2018 | Designed by Liz Dresner
The artist used gouache on paper to create these illustrations.
Printed in China by RR Donnelley Asia Printing Solutions Ltd.,
Dongguan City, Guangdong Province

10  9  8  7  6  5  4  3  2  1